W9-APL-271

A New True Book

SOUTH AFRICA

By Karen Jacobsen

Flag of South Africa

CHILDRENS PRESS®
CHICAGO

Mother and child from the Ndebele tribe

PHOTO CREDITS

©Cameramann International Ltd.—10 (left), 31, 32 (right), 37

Historical Pictures Service, Chicago—22, 24, 28, 29 (2 photos)

© Jason Lauré—15 (bottom left), 16, 33, 42

Odyssey Productions—© Robert Frerck, 8 (left), 12 (right top & bottom), 19 (2 photos), 34 (right), 36, 38

Photri—© J. Allen Cash, 9 (left), 17 (top left), 18 (left & right), 34 (left), 41, 45

Root Resources—© John Hoellen, 4, 10 (right); © Byron Crader, 17 (right & bottom left), 26

Tom Stack & Associates—© Alan G. Nelson, 12 (left); © C. Benjamin, 18 (center), 39; © F. S. Mitchell, 20

SuperStock International, Inc.—Cover, 2, 44 (2 photos)

Tony Stone Worldwide-Click/Chicago— © Berlitz, 8 (right), 15 (bottom right)

Valen—© Fred Bruemmer, 7; © Joyce Photographics, 9 (right), 32 (left); © Klaus Werner, 15 (top right); © Peter Holland, 15 (top left)

Al Magnus—6 (map)

Len W. Meents—maps 7, 9, 11,

Cover — Green Point and Sea Point area, Cape Town, South Africa

Library of Congress Cataloging-in-Publication Data

Jacobsen, Karen.
    South Africa / by Karen Jacobsen.
        p.   cm. — (A New true book)
    Includes index.
    Summary: Discusses South Africa's geography, history, people. government, and anti-apartheid movement.
    ISBN 0-516-01176-6
    1.   South Africa—Juvenile literature.
[1.   South Africa.]   I.   Title.
DT753.J33   1989   89-10044
968—dc20   CIP
                                         AC

TABLE OF CONTENTS

Cape of Good Hope, South Africa

THE LAND

South Africa is in the southern half of the world. South Africa is the southernmost country on the continent of Africa.

South Africa lies between the Atlantic Ocean and the Indian Ocean. The two great bodies of water meet at the Cape of Good Hope. Ships and sailors must "round the Cape" in order to follow the southern sea route around Africa.

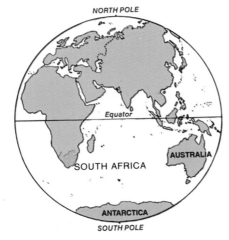

South Africa is south of the equator.

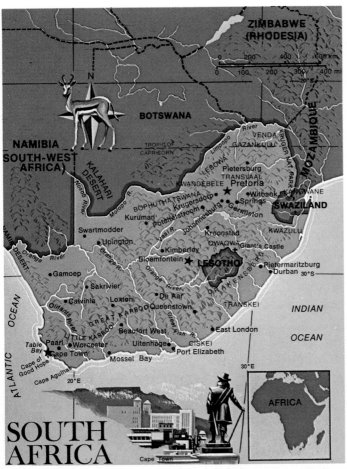

The countries of Namibia, Botswana, Zimbabwe, Swaziland, and Mozambique form the northern border of South Africa. The small country of Lesotho is inside South Africa. Lesotho is independent and has its own government.

THE PROVINCES

South Africa is a republic with three capital cities and four provinces. The largest province is the Cape of Good Hope Province. Its capital city, Cape Town, is the home of South Africa's Parliament. Cape Town is the country's oldest city and an important modern seaport.

Cape Town is the capital city of the Cape of Good Hope Province.

The Transvaal is a large inland province. Its capital city, Pretoria, is the home of South Africa's government offices. Pretoria is a major business center. Kruger National Park in eastern Transvaal is the natural home of many native African animals.

Parliament House (below) in Pretoria, the capital of Transvaal, and zebras grazing in Kruger National Park (right)

Homes of black farm workers (above)
and Bloemfontein (right),
the capital city of
the Orange Free State

Orange Free State,
another inland province, is
world-famous for its diamond
and uranium mines.
Bloemfontein, the capital
city of Orange Free State, is
the home of South Africa's
national law courts.

Durban (above and right)
is a busy seaport on
the Indian Ocean. There
are separate beaches
for each racial group.

Natal is South Africa's
east coast province. Its
major city is Durban, an
industrial and resort center.
Natal has some of South
Africa's most beautiful
beaches.

TRIBAL HOMELANDS

Several areas, called tribal homelands, have been set up inside South Africa. The South African government wants all the blacks in the country to move into the homelands. The government says the homelands are

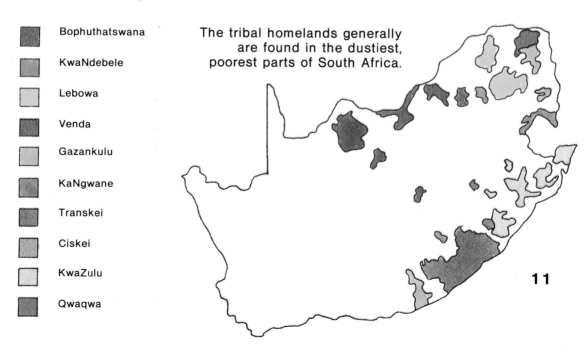

Bophuthatswana

KwaNdebele

Lebowa

Venda

Gazankulu

KaNgwane

Transkei

Ciskei

KwaZulu

Qwaqwa

The tribal homelands generally are found in the dustiest, poorest parts of South Africa.

The blacks do not want
to move to the
homelands set
aside for them
by the South
African government.

independent countries and
not part of South Africa.
Most black South Africans
do not want to live in these
tribal homelands.

APARTHEID

Forcing people to move to these "homelands" far from their real homes is legal in South Africa. It is part of a government plan called apartheid. Apartheid means "apartness" in Afrikaans, the language of many white South Africans.

Apartheid laws keep the races completely apart. Apartheid laws keep white people in power.

THE PEOPLE OF SOUTH AFRICA

Nearly 32 million people live in South Africa today. Apartheid laws divide these people into four racial groups: white, African, Colored, and Asian.

White: 4.8 million
Colored: 2.8 million
Asian: 0.9 million
African: 23+ million

Most white South Africans are the descendants of Dutch settlers from Holland or English settlers from

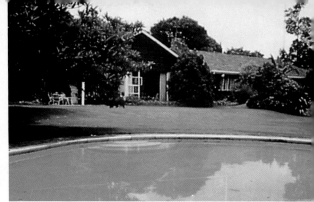

Attending
horseraces (above left),
bowling on the
green (left), and
living in homes with
pools and servants
are part of the
white South African's
life-style.

Britain. The Dutch
descendants are known as
Afrikaners. White South
Africans live very well in
"white only" areas. They own
and control almost
everything in South Africa. **15**

"Africans" are the black people whose ancestors originally lived in Africa. Many black South Africans live in "townships" built outside white South African towns and cities. Black South Africans may work for whites, but they may not live in "white only" areas.

Soweto is a black township twenty miles from Johannesburg.

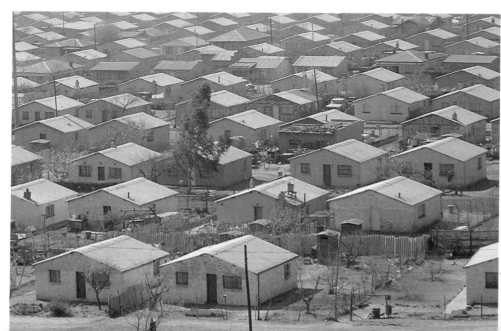

The Zulus are the largest tribe in South Africa. Some still live in small villages called kraals (left).

Most black South Africans are members of African tribes. They speak their tribal languages and follow some of the traditions. Only a small number are able to live as their people did long ago.

The Colored people of South Africa are forced to live, work, and play in segregated areas.

Colored South Africans are people with both white and African ancestors. The apartheid laws force the Colored South Africans to live in special areas. Colored South Africans may go to school only with other Colored South Africans.

Asian South Africans are the descendants of Indian servants and laborers who came to South Africa in the 1860s. Apartheid laws force Asian South Africans to live apart from the other races. They must live in special Asian sections of South African cities.

Asians, such as this Indian storekeeper (left), are also segregated.

EARLY HISTORY

The first tribes in the
southern part of Africa were
the San, or Bushmen, and
the Khoikhoi, or Hottentots.
The San were skilled hunters.
The Khoikhoi raised cattle
and sheep. The early people
lived in a paradise of plenty.

The Khoikhoi (or Hottentots) and San (Bushmen)
people were the first to settle in South Africa.
Their rock drawings can still be seen.

By the time Europeans arrived, tribes that spoke Bantu languages had moved into the eastern part of South Africa.

In 1652, the first white settlers from Holland arrived at the Cape. They set up a station to supply passing ships. In time more Dutch settlers came. The settlers took land from the tribes, sometimes by force. Many tribal people were killed or died of diseases. Others became servants or moved away into the wilderness.

Zulu warriors prepare for battle.

The Zulus began as a small tribe living in the eastern part of southern Africa. In the late 1700s the Zulus became very powerful. Their leader was King Shaka. He built a strong warrior kingdom. Shaka's Zulu warriors defeated every other tribe. The white settlers stayed away from the Zulus.

THE NINETEENTH CENTURY

After the defeat of Napoleon in Europe, the Dutch had to give their South African colony to Britain. British settlers began to arrive in Cape Town in 1820. Soon after, the English language and English law became official in the Cape Colony. The Dutch settlers had no power and did not like the British.

Dutch or Afrikaner farmers moved to the
Transvaal to get away from the British.

Starting in the 1830s,
many hundreds of Afrikaner
farmers—called *Boers* in
Afrikaans—decided to leave
the British Cape Colony.
They formed wagon trains
and headed north to find
new lands for themselves.

In Natal the Boers fought the powerful Zulus, led by King Dingane. At first the Zulus won. But finally Boer guns defeated the Zulu spears.

The Zulus also ruled the land north of Natal called Zululand. In 1878 the Zulus went to war with the British. The Zulus won a big battle at Isandhlwana. But in 1879 their king, Cetshwayo, was forced to surrender to the British. Zululand came under British rule.

The Boers wanted to keep their Dutch religion and customs alive. Many of their homes were built in the Dutch style

The Boers cleared the land and planted crops. They used slave labor.

The British started sugar plantations along the coast. Because slavery was not legal in British colonies, the British planters brought in more workers from India.

DIAMONDS AND GOLD

In 1870 a boy found a large, glassy stone near Kimberley. It was a diamond. Word spread, and fortune hunters came from all around the world to find diamonds in South Africa.

In 1886, South Africa's gold was discovered near Johannesburg. Hoping to strike it rich, more fortune hunters poured into the Transvaal to dig for gold.

THE ANGLO-BOER WAR

The Boers wanted complete control of the Transvaal's government and riches for themselves. They wanted the British and all the other fortune hunters to get out of South Africa.

In 1899 the Boers attacked the British Army at

The Boers attacked the British at Mafeking.

The Boer army (left) was not as well supplied as the British forces. Some Boers (right) were herded into the church square in Pretoria.

the Transvaal border. At first the Boers won some battles. But the British had more men and supplies.

The Anglo-Boer War was bitter and bloody. In 1902, the Boers surrendered to the British.

At the end of the war, the

British were very hard on the Boers. But later the two old enemies agreed to share in governing South Africa. In 1910, Transvaal, Orange Free State, Natal, and Cape of Good Hope Province became the Union of South Africa, a part of the British Empire.

In World War I and World War II, both Afrikaner and English South Africans fought at Britain's side to defeat Germany.

TWO SOUTH AFRICAS

Today, the descendants of Dutch and British settlers still govern South Africa. Each group keeps its own customs.

Afrikaans and English are both official languages. White South African children must learn both languages in school. Signs are written in both languages.

Student crossing guards at an Afrikaans school

Johannesburg (right) is a business center. It is run by the whites (above) who control the economic and social life of the city.

South Africa is a world leader in mining, banking, and other business activities. For the whites, South Africa is a beautiful and comfortable place to live.

But there is another South
Africa. It is the South Africa
of the black, Colored, and
Asian South Africans.
Because of apartheid, they
are not free. Their South
Africa is a hard and often
cruel place to live.

Black miners (right) and servants work for the whites, but they can never live where white people live.

There are very few jobs for black South Africans in the places where they live. To earn a living, black workers must travel far from their homes.

Many work in the gold and

diamond mines. The mine shafts are deep under the ground. There is always a great danger of flooding or cave-ins.

Other black South Africans make day trips into the white South African areas. There they work for very low wages. They work as servants in the homes of whites or in white-owned businesses. Under apartheid it is a crime for blacks to stay overnight in "whites only" areas.

EDUCATION IN SOUTH AFRICA

In South Africa all of the government schools and most of the private schools are segregated by race and language.

In the free government schools, white English students and white Afrikaner

Signs are written in both Afrikaans and English.

whites
blankes

Primary school in Johannesburg, South Africa

students are taught in their
own language in grades 1
to 6. They learn the other
official language in grades 7
to 10.

Nursery school in Soweto

Colored and Asian students have their own separate schools. Classes are usually taught in English. Some students are given special permission to attend white private schools, if their families can afford the tuition.

Black students between the ages of 6 to 15 go to public schools. Black students are taught in black languages and Afrikaans.

The public schools are crowded. Most black students drop out of school after a few

Bantu school on a ranch near Victoria West in South Africa

years. Others live in places where there are no schools.

In the early 1980s only about 20 percent of South Africa's black children went to school.

Even so, every year many black South Africans finish high school. Some of the most outstanding black students even manage to graduate from college.

In South Africa, the state universities also are segregated. There are five white English, five white

Cape Town University

Afrikaans, one Colored, one Asian, and five black universities. Only the most outstanding students of other races have ever been accepted to study at the white English universities.

Desmond Tutu (center) was the first black Anglican bishop of Johannesburg. He was awarded the Nobel Peace Prize in 1984 for his efforts to bring nonviolent change to South Africa.

ANTI-APARTHEID ACTIVITY

Most black South Africans want to end apartheid. They want the right to vote and make their own laws.

Some want to use peaceful means to win their rights, but others are willing to use force to gain their freedom.

Because of apartheid, many countries will not do business with South Africa. They will not permit their citizens to be in sporting events with South African athletes. The United Nations has condemned apartheid and South Africa.

These anti-apartheid actions are having an effect. South Africa is losing money. Many white South Africans are moving to other countries. Other white South

Until the government can find a peaceful way to bring the blacks and the whites together, the future of South Africa is uncertain.

Africans are beginning to see that they must make changes at home or they may lose everything.

The Republic of South Africa is the wealthiest and most modern country in Africa. White South Africans are among the best-educated people in the world. Yet, the

South Africa is a beautiful land that is rich in natural resources.

future of South Africa is
very uncertain.

Can South Africa become
a land of freedom and
fairness for all its people?

Will there be peace or
more violence?

Can South Africa save
itself?

WORDS YOU SHOULD KNOW

Africa(AFF • rih • ka) — the large continent south of Europe

ancestor(AN • sess • ter) — a grandparent or blood relation earlier in history

cape(KAYP) — a point of land on a coastline

capital(KAP • ih • til) — a city in which a country's government is located

cause(KAWZ) — a purpose; a position or side in a dispute

Cetshwayo(ketch • WHY • o) — the king of the Zulus who was defeated by the British in 1879

colony(KAHL • uh • nee) — a settlement of people from another country

condemn(kun • DEM) — declare to be wrong

continent (KAHN • tih • nent) — a large landmass on the earth

equator(ih • KWAY • ter) — an imaginary line around the earth, equally distant from the North and South poles

fortune(FOR • chun) — good (or bad) luck

independent(in • dih • PEN • dint) — not controlled by another person or country

inland(IN • land) — without or not near a coastline

Isandhlwana(ee • sahn • jil • WHA • nah) — the place where Zulu warriors defeated the British Army in 1878

legal(LEE • gil) — according to the law

mine shaft(MYNE • SHAFT) — an entrance or a tunnel in a mine

native(NAY • tiv) — born in or belonging to a place

paradise(PAIR • uh • dice) — a heavenly place

parliament(PAR • lih • ment) — the law-making body of some governments

plantation(plan • TAY • shun) — a farm; a place for growing crops

province(PRAH • vince) — a state or section of a country

republic(rih • PUB • lick) — a country with elected leaders

resort(rih • ZORT) — a popular vacation place
skillful(SKIL • full) — having expert ability
station(STAY • shun) — a regular stopping place
tradition(tra • DIH • shun) — an old custom
tribe(TRYBE) — a group of people related by blood and customs
violence(VILE • ence) — attacks that cause severe injuries to
       people or property
wilderness(WIL • der • niss) — a region not inhabited by people

INDEX

About the Author

Karen Jacobsen is a graduate of the University of Connecticut and Syracuse University. She has been a teacher and is a writer. She likes to find out about interesting subjects and then write about them.